704

# A Dog's
# Night Before
# Christmas

written by **Henry Beard**
created by **John Boswell**
illustrated by **Susann Ferris Jones**

A JOHN BOSWELL ASSOCIATES BOOK

BROADWAY BOOKS   NEW YORK

'Twas the night before Christmas,
and all through the house,
Not a creature was stirring,
except for a mouse.

I awoke with a start from the deepest of sleeps,
My slumbers disrupted by shrill little peeps.

From the ruckus it kicked up in its tiny nest,
The rodent was hosting a holiday fest.

But mice aren't my problem—that's work for the cat,
Though I'd tear it to pieces if it were a rat.
'Tis a subtle distinction no human quite gets,
A division of labor among household pets.

'Tis why parrots won't fetch things, and goldfish don't talk,
And hamsters don't beg to go out for a walk,
And the reason 'twas always a job for the pooch
To ransack the household for goodies to mooch.

So off through the place I went busily nosing,
While snug under duvets the family was dozing.
(Thanks to false accusations that yours truly sheds,
And that frame-up for fleabites, I'm banished from beds.)

From the mantel hung stockings I'd happily chew up,
But that seemed to me like a serious screwup,

As bad as that time when from sheer force of habit,
I happened to gobble the neighbor's pet rabbit.

I confess I was tempted to go help myself
To the plateful of cookies they'd left on the shelf,

But I wasn't too eager to get into Dutch
For some measly Fig Newtons I don't like that much.

At the front of the parlor they'd set up a spruce—
A nice place to pee, though I doubt that's its use.
They laugh when they see me retrieving a stick,
Then they drag home a tree with a trunk a foot thick.

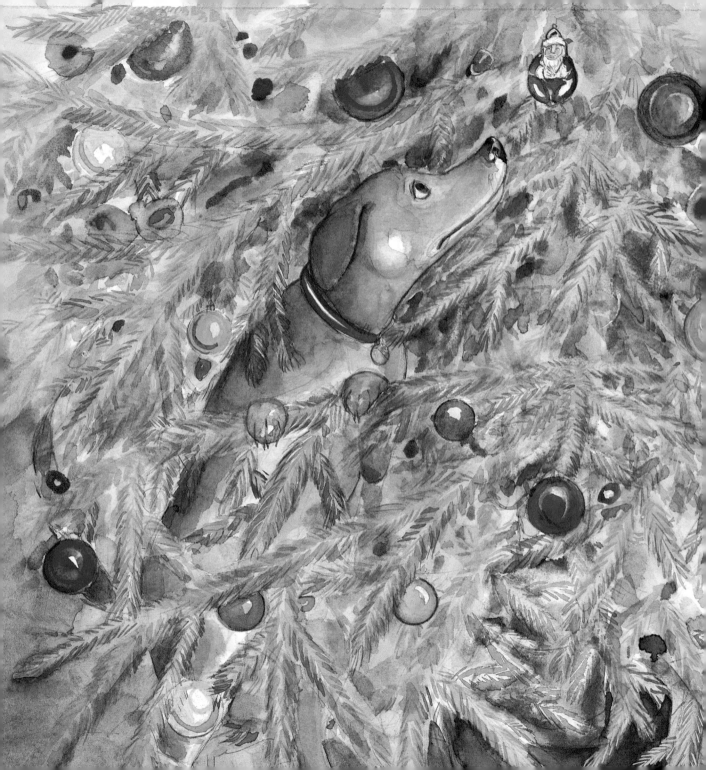

They'd draped it with doodads and tinsel in swirls—
I'd have liked it much more if they'd kept a few squirrels,
And instead of the boxes piled up at its base,
'Twere a couple of pigeons a puppy could chase.

I sniffed through the kitchen in search of a treat,
A tidbit of cheese or a morsel of meat.

But any choice scraps had been swept from the floor,
And the garbage was bagged up outside the back door.

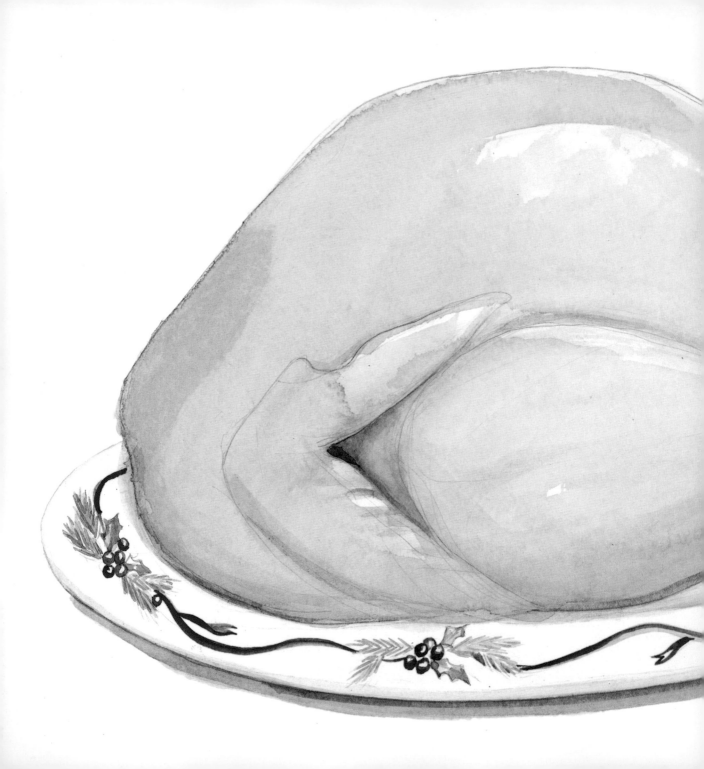

As all 'round the room I continued to prowl,
I spied on the counter a huge frozen fowl.
They say 'tis a bird, but that thing's never flown,
And in that whole hulk there's not one decent bone.

If you want my opinion, I'd say, lose the turkey—
Let's have bacon and pizza and lots of beef jerky,
And cupcakes and popcorn and apple brown betty,
And a nice heaping plateful of day-old spaghetti!

Some meatballs and tacos and slices of brisket,
Chop suey and chili and a gravy-soaked biscuit,

And donuts and dumplings and hot dogs and ham,
A big bag of jellybeans, a whole leg of lamb!

But you can't dine on dreams, so I'd nothing to nibble,
Aside from some bites of that horrible kibble.
I was searching the sofa for any lost toys
When from high on the housetop I heard a loud noise.

A burglar? A goblin? A rabid raccoon?
A bug-eyed space monster from Mars or the Moon?

A flesh-eating zombie? A goon with a gun?
A bloodthirsty psycho? A con on the run?

With my heart in my mouth, I crept up to the attic;
Confronting a foe can be very traumatic.

I tiptoed to the dormer and peered through the casement—
I was ready to fight or to head for the basement.

Then I saw such a scene in the snow on the roof
That for once I was truly too tongue-tied to woof.
Kitty-corner there slalomed a sleigh drawn by pusses,
A tabby toboggan performing deft schusses.

And perched on the rear of that cat-sled there sat
A stout Saint Bernard in a trim Alpine hat,

With a pipe in his mouth and a cask on his collar.
He reined in his mousers, and I heard him holler—

"Whoa *Misty*, whoa *Smokey*, whoa *Nosey* and *Chloe*!
Whoa *Gypsy*, and *Frisky*, and *Whiskey*, and *Zoe*!
Whoa *Molly*, and *Polly*, and *Muffin*, and *Fluffy*!
Whoa *Dusty*, and *Rusty*, and *Ruffles*, and *Scruffy*!"

I was starting to think this must be Santa Claws
When he tapped on the floorboards with one of his paws,
And a pack of Chihuahuas jumped out of the back,
And each of them carried a fat gunnysack.

They yipped and they yapped as they mounted the slope,
And climbed to the chimney and tossed up a rope.
They shinnied their way to the top of the flue,
And hopped in the vent-hole and vanished from view.

I dashed down the stairs, and I raced through the hall.
I rushed to the fireplace, and there by the wall,
They'd laid out a banquet—a full groaning board,
A scrumptious buffet crammed with foods I adored.

I ran to the window in time to catch sight
Of that marvelous mastiff before he took flight.
Then as he ascended, he waved from his seat,
*"Merry Christmas!"* he yodeled, *"and bon appétit!"*

**B**
**BROADWAY**

A DOG'S NIGHT BEFORE CHRISTMAS. Copyright © 2005 by John Boswell Management, Inc. All rights reserved. No part of this book may be reproduced or transmitted in any form or by any means, electronic or mechanical, including photocopying, recording, or by any information storage and retrieval system, without written permission from the publisher. For information, address Broadway Books, a division of Random House, Inc.

PRINTED IN CHINA

BROADWAY BOOKS and its logo, a letter B bisected on the diagonal, are trademarks of Random House, Inc.

Visit our Web site at www.broadwaybooks.com

First edition published 2005

Book design **by** *Nan Jernigan*

LIBRARY OF CONGRESS CATALOGING-IN-PUBLICATION DATA
Beard, Henry.
A dog's night before Christmas / written by Henry Beard ; created by John Boswell ; illustrated by Susann Ferris Jones.
    p. cm.
    (alk. paper)
 1. Dogs—Juvenile poetry. 2. Christmas—Juvenile poetry. 3. Children's poetry, American.    I. Boswell, John. II. Jones, Susann Ferris. III. Title.
  PS3552.E165D64 2005
  811'.54—dc22

2005045701

ISBN 0-7679-1852-5
10 9 8 7 6 5 4 3 2 1